How to Explore the Amazon

Contents

Badger LEARNING

Vocabulary

acai	machete
balsa wood	paralyse
caiman	piranhas
diseases	poisonous
guava	toucans

The Amazon is amazing!

It is one of the wildest places on Earth.

In the thick jungle you might see a howler monkey, a man-eating fish or a deadly crocodile.

1. Getting ready

Before you go, you must check out websites and books about the Amazon.

You should also get some maps of the Amazon region.

South America

Venezuela

Colombia

Ecuador

Brazil

Peru

Bolivia

Pacific ocean

Atlantic ocean

Amazon rainforest

Next, find out where you can hire a jungle guide.

It's a good idea to learn some of the local language.

Languages spoken in the Amazon:

Country	Language
Brazil	Portuguese
Peru	Spanish
Bolivia	Spanish
Ecuador	Spanish

What to take

The weather will be hot and very wet so take clothes that will be cool to wear and will dry off quickly.

Don't take too much! Try to make sure everything can do more than one job.

A plastic sheet could also be used as a tent or a raincoat.

You will also need:
- a backpack
- strong boots
- a hat
- a camera

You can buy some things for your trip when you get to the Amazon.

You will need a machete to:
- hack your way through the thick forest
- cut wood for building your shelter

2. Food

You should pack lots of dried food, like pasta and rice.

There is plenty of water to cook it!

You can catch some fish to eat with your pasta and rice.

You don't need a rod to catch fish in the Amazon.

There are so many fish you will just need a line and some fish hooks.

Look out for piranhas!

You will need to put some wire on the end of your line so their sharp teeth can't bite through your fishing line.

You can find fruit to eat in the Amazon.

Some of the fruit grows high up in the trees and you will have to climb up to get it.

What fruits grow in the Amazon?
- Guava
- Acai berries
- Wild avocado
- Passion fruit

If you are lucky, you may find fruit on the forest floor.

How will you know if it is safe to eat the fruit?

Look out for monkey bite marks in the fruit.

If the fruit has monkey bite marks, there is a good chance that it will be safe for humans to eat.

What else can you eat?
Some palm trees have a white pulp inside. This is called palm heart.

Top tip for cutting out palm hearts
Always cut with the blade of the machete away from you. Palm tree trunks are very hard and your blade could bounce off and hit you in the leg.

3. Travelling by river

You will have a lot of stuff to carry and it is very hard to walk through the rainforest, so the best way to travel is by river.

You could make a raft out of balsa wood. You can find balsa wood logs by the river edges.

Balsa wood logs are light enough to pick up and you can easily cut them to the right length with your machete.

Watch out!

Don't step on a stingray. It could stab you with its poisonous tail. The pain is awful. You might not be able to walk for a week.

Crocodiles

The black caiman crocodile is very dangerous. It can grow up to five metres long.

It grabs hold of an animal and drowns it because its teeth are better at holding than at tearing.

4. Amazon dangers

It's not just the big animals you have to look out for. The insects in the Amazon are terrible.

- They can bite through your clothes.
- Their bites itch and can give you diseases.
- You should always sleep under a net at night.

Look out for:

- black flies – tiny biting flies that hang around the rivers

- sweat bees – small bees that swarm around you and lick the salt in your sweat

- wolf spiders – spiders that can paralyse your arm if they bite

Look out for storms!

A thunderstorm can suddenly brew up. The strong wind snaps branches off the trees.

In just a few minutes the jungle river can become a dangerous flood.

5. Animals in the Amazon

The Amazon is not a quiet place.

The animals in the Amazon can be very noisy.

Amazon noises:

- the squealing of the howler monkeys
- the squawking of the parrots
- the screeching of the toucans

Look out for spider monkeys.

These monkeys go around in groups of up to 50.

If you copy their squealing food calls, they will call back

Watch out!
These monkeys can get angry and throw branches at you… or try to wee and poo on you.

Peccaries

You will smell these animals before you see them!

They stink like sweat.

Then you will hear the clicking of their tusks as they root through the fallen leaves for food.

There may be 500 peccaries in a herd and, if they see or smell you, they may charge.

Your only escape is to find a tree you can climb and get up it quickly.

Jungle heaven or jungle hell?

The rainforest is beautiful but it can also be deadly.

- A spider can paralyse you with one bite.
- Dangerous floods can wash you away.
- Spider monkeys can poo on you.

If you are going to survive a trip to the Amazon you need to be strong.

Are you up for it?

Questions

Where is the Amazon? *(page 5)*

What languages are spoken in the Amazon? *(page 7)*

What type of food should you pack? *(page 12)*

How can you tell if fruit is safe to eat? *(page 16)*

Name three animals you need to look out for in the Amazon. *(pages 19-28)*

Would you take a trip to the Amazon?

Index